Memories of a
Jewish Childhood

HARRIET OTTENSTEIN

EDITED BY:
DAVID ABRAMOWITZ

ISBN: 1466456515
ISBN 13: 9781466456518

Dedications

Nathan Ottenstein (Papa) at 90.

To **Nathan Ottenstein**, my father, who kept his Jewish identity regardless of whether it was fashionable or not or whether it marked him as different. When he found himself in social environments that could have made it difficult to hold fast to his faith, he held on tighter still. This book is borne of an old-fashioned Judaism and my father's strength to say exactly who and what he was without apology to either Christian or Jew. This book would never have been written if it had not been for Papa.

To **Dora Rosenfeld**, who is a shining example of a "woman of valor." She continues to be a role model of strength and determination for life. Her acts of loving kindness are inspirational. She gave a home to the homeless who were despaired of spirit; those brutalized loners who survived the Holocaust and had no families to call their own she took in without hesitation. She is immortalized in this book. May her life and legacy be for a blessing.

Mrs. Rosenfeld has asked that, along with her name, the name of my mother—her dear friend, Joan Ottenstein—be remembered as the first person who welcomed her to the neighborhood when she was a stranger in a strange land. My mother extended her own love, kindness, and friendship to Mrs. Rosenfeld, and their friendship was forged forever.

*Dora Grunfeld-Rosenfeld...photographed about 1947
at the displaced persons camp,which was in the Cloisters,
in Ettal, Germany near Wasserburg.*

Contents

Acknowledgments

To my childhood friend, Linda Sawello-Klappholz, who "raised me up on eagles' wings" numerous times throughout my life, starting in childhood. I am deeply appreciative. Her sympathy in bad times, her laughter in good times, and always her keen mind make ours a special, life-long friendship.

Thanks are due to Aunt Thelma Ottenstein, Cousin Barry Ottenstein, and Claire Ottenstein-Ross, my sister-in-law, for providing much encouragement, enthusiasm, and praise during our long telephone conversations, and for listening to the stories.

Thanks are due to my longtime friend Fred Batt who by his praise through cyberspace for my writing inspired me to see this book to fruition.

Special thanks to Juan Cuevas for his belief in my writing and his confidence in the successful outcome of my endeavor.

I am grateful to my supportive editor, David Abramowitz, for his meticulous review of this book, for his skilled technical computer assistance, and his scrupulous reading and re-reading of the manuscript. I thank him for being there for me and for sharing his sensitive comments and impressions. His encouragement sustained me through the completion of this writing. His enthusiasm, generosity of time, and talent helped make this book not only a possibility but a reality.

Finally, I want to thank my family, for enduring the long stretches of time when I was writing and off in a 1950s world, some of which was personally painful and emotionally draining. To all of my children and grandson—Alicia, Juan, Victoria, Tor, Adrian, Andre, Daniel, and Nathan — I give a heartfelt thank you for being sensitive, attentive listeners. The stories in this book are your heritage, borne of past generations' toils, tears, laughter, and joys.

Preface

The Holocaust had a far-reaching psychological impact on the new Jewish generation growing up in the 1950's. The goal of my book is to open a window on how it was to live in a close-knit Jewish community—a type of community that does not exist anymore. Some stories are funny ethnic tales that will resonate with the generation that grew up in the east-coast urban cities in New York and New Jersey. The reader will find stories that are purely nostalgic word pictures; others are dark and disturbing Holocaust narratives. In "The Sunflowers," the reader will be confronted with blatant anti-Semitism expressed in an American neighborhood and public school. The anti-Semitism was aimed toward a helpless child with few coping skills. I was that child.

In this book are the stories, sights, and events that formed my perception of being a Jew.

Harriet Ottenstein
November 2011

Author's Notes

"Why 18 Chapters?"

The Hebrew word for life is חי (*chai*). It has a numerical value of 18. This book contains 18 chapters. This number affirms the determination of our people to keep our heritage and religion alive in the face of ages of generations who sought our destruction. We are admonished in our prayer books, "Choose life!" and to that I say,

"L'Chaim!"

"Scenes from Childhood"

Subtitles have been inspired by the famous piano collection, *Scenes From Childhood*, by Romantic composer, Robert Schumann. His thirteen piece anthology was written as adult reflections and subtle hint reminiscences of childhood past. The collection was intended for adults to play for their children. It is the author's wish that this literary collection will also be the legacy of parents to give or read to their children as appropriate ages allow.

"G-d" and "L-rd"

It has been my personal choice to have taken the traditional practice for Jews to write "G-d" and "L-rd" by replacing the "o" with a dash. Although, many Jews have concluded that a secular use of the name of the Holy One is no longer tethered to Talmudic or later rulings. My childhood memories impact upon the person I am now, and my personal choice is bound in these pages.

Scenes from Childhood

Scenes from Childhood

Schav

The kitchen seemed to glow in the white light that streamed through the open summer windows. Outside it was baking hot, and inside the kitchen, the air was almost steamy. The screened door that had let me in failed to provide any relief from the heat. I could smell the good smells and feel the love and happiness enveloping me in the hot room. A place waited for me at the table.

Auntie Dora poured precious white sorrel soup called *schav* from a ladle into almost-flat soup bowls. I was only four years old, but I could feel the love and contentment in her gaze as she looked down at me. We all loved Auntie Dora, her soup, and her kitchen.

Leon, her son, sat at the table to my left as we eagerly slurped our cool schav from the flat bowls. The grownups around us—Auntie Bertha across from me and Uncle Alex, whom Leon secretly named Schloima—held adoring eyes on us, watching us the way people take delight in a puppy lapping up milk. We were objects of sheer wonder to them.

We were objects of sheer wonder to them.

"Auntie Dora," I asked, "Why do you have numbers written on your arm? You have them, too, Auntie Bertha."

In an instant, the room hardened and an atmosphere of discomfort and strain settled around us. Auntie Bertha said something to Auntie Dora in Romanian, avoiding Yiddish because we children understood a little of it. Romanian was the adults' secret language they used when children were not supposed to understand.

Leon echoed my question. "Mommy, why do you have those numbers on your arm?"

The question hung in the humid kitchen like a dark cloud in a windless sky, hovering over us laden with meanings we had yet to understand. Auntie Dora's eyes stared blankly straight ahead. She seemed to look through the kitchen wall, her gaze stretching far, far away. How could we have known that her gaze looked down an invisible road that led to haunting horrors of sights and smells that no living creature should have ever had to experience?

She took a slow, deep breath and looked with searching eyes from us to Auntie Bertha, whose own eyes were wide open.

With an almost imperceptible shake of her head, Auntie Bertha blurted out, "Don't tell them."

At that moment, my own mother appeared at the door, lit by the white light. Auntie Bertha's "don't tell them" still hung suspended in the air. Everything in that moment seemed suspended. Even our slurping stopped as we looked up from our flat bowls and waited for Auntie Dora's reply.

I will never forget the tone of her voice. How could a voice be so soft and hard at the same time? "It was my address in Germany," she said finally.

With the insensitivity of childhood, Leon pushed on. "Mommy, you couldn't remember your address? You had to write it on yourself?"

I saw Auntie Dora's eyes fill with tears. She swallowed hard. "Those numbers were put on me so I would never forget."

Scenes from Childhood

The Religious Lesson

One day Papa and I went for a walk to the hardware store three blocks from our house. We had to watch our step; the roots of the ancient oaks and maple trees that lined the cobblestone street had pushed up from below the pavement, heaving the sidewalk into a crooked, bumpy path to our destination. We passed the shoemaker's shop near the corner, but Papa didn't go inside to get his shoes shined as he sometimes did, to sit in one of the big leather chairs inside the booths with wooden gates. I glanced into the shop as we passed and saw the old shoemaker toiling over his shoes. The pleasant smell of shoe polish and leather wafted out into the heavy air of summer.

We continued down the street, passing the gypsies who lived in stores and hung colorful but unmatched sheets and curtains over the storefront windows for privacy. I found the gypsies interesting, but I didn't tell Papa so. Papa told me to hold his hand and stay close until we had passed the gypsies and arrived at the hardware store.

The hardware store was as hot as an oven. Its dry, almost-gray, dusty oak floor badly needed to be waxed. Old, black ceiling fans hung from the ornately carved tin ceiling and quivered, shook, and buzzed as they stirred the air in the seemingly airless store. On both the left and right, the walls were hung with huge metal bins that almost touched the ceiling. The bins were full of nails, screws, and bolts of various sizes, with large metal scoops for digging up helpings of hardware, which were then poured into the hanging scales that dangled above my head. Nails, screws, and bolts were sold by the pound back then, not in packages and boxes. Besides the hardware, there were ironing boards, galvanized buckets, scrubbing boards, clothespins, washtubs, and hoses. It wasn't the sort of store a girl child was eager to go to, but at least it was something to do on an oppressively hot day in the city.

Two olive-skinned young brothers with curly hair, dark eyes, and long lashes lived in a room in the back of the store. I could see into the room from the counter. They, too, had a colorful curtain strung along the opening to their living area behind the store. They were perched on tall stools with their heads bent down, wearing their *yarmulkes* (Jewish skullcaps) and studying the Talmud.

The boys came reluctantly to the counter. I thought they had the saddest, most serious faces I'd ever seen. I would hate to sit in that boring store all day long, surrounded by hard and ugly things, and have to study from those big books in Hebrew with no pictures at all. I must have been staring at one of the boys, because he gave me a quick smile before asking Papa how he could help him.

Papa had come to buy mezuzahs. Mezuzot (the proper plural of the word) are little metal or wooden boxes containing prayers that are affixed to every doorpost in a Jewish home, except the bathroom. Inside each mezuzah is a tiny, perfectly handwritten parchment scroll.

Papa told the boys what he wanted and asked them if the mezuzahs were strictly kosher, meaning perfect without mistakes. I hoped they were, so we could leave the store, get outside to some fresh air, and maybe even have an ice cream cone on the way home. I was about to burst from some form of suffocation or exasperation called boredom.

Papa took his time buying some little nails for the mezuzahs and inspecting everything. (He didn't use the correct Hebrew plural—mezuzot—so I never learned the right way to refer to the plural.) The mezuzahs the boys offered him were made of thin metal, costing only pennies. I wondered if the boys themselves were the scribes who had made and written on the scrolls inside. Why did Papa have such interest in these awful screws and nails? He was searching for a certain size, a special one, for something or other. I was thinking impatiently of my friend Leon and how I was going to tell him to never, ever go to the hardware store. It was torture.

I don't remember how, but finally we left the store and walked home. I probably got my ice cream cone, because Papa usually bought me one when we went out together for a walk. Papa stopped by the Rosenfeld's apartment and told me to play with Leon for a while. Just as Leon and I were settling down to watch *The Lone Ranger* on television, Papa asked Uncle Louie to show us the mezuzah he wore around his neck. Uncle Louie proudly opened his shirt to let us see it. I can still picture it to this day— exquisite gold worked in exotic filigree. He let us come close enough to peek through the little holes in the filigree work and glimpse the tiny scroll. He told us that the prayer inside the mezuzah was the oldest and most holy prayer of all. He said that only boys could wear a mezuzah and that it had to be worn inside the shirt, close to the heart. It wasn't meant for others to see.

Papa changed the subject rather abruptly and asked Uncle Louie, "So what's doing with those two boys in the hardware store?"

Uncle Louie said that only one relative had been found for them here in America. He told Papa that the boys were all alone in this world except for that relative—an uncle perhaps—who had set them up running the store. Aside from him, they were on their own. Their parents and all their relatives had died in the Holocaust.

"Poor boys." Papa shook his head, pondering the fate of the two young men.

"One thing about us," Uncle Louie said, "is that we always provide trades for our sons; maybe even two trades, just in case one doesn't work out." Papa nodded sadly in agreement, and Uncle Louie turned to Leon and me. "Remember, when you come into the house and when you go out, touch the mezuzah with respect. The scroll inside says, 'Hear, O Israel! The L-rd, our G-d, is one. You shall love your Eternal

G-d with all your mind, with all your strength, with all your being."

I decided not to tell Leon about the boring hardware store.

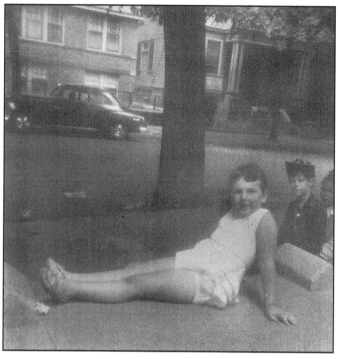

Peshine Avenue, Newark, New Jersey.

Tisha B'Av—Child Falling Asleep

This story is entitled "Tisha B'Av," which is the ninth day of Av, a month in the Jewish calendar that usually falls in August. It is a significant date in Jewish history because it is clearly the saddest date on the Jewish calendar, and it is marked as a solemn day of mourning. In 1190, the entire Jewish population of York, England was massacred on Tisha B'Av. On Tisha B'Av in 1492, King Ferdinand and Queen Isabella ordered the expulsion of the Jews from Spain; any who remained *were given the choice to convert to Christianity or be burned alive at the stake. On Tisha B'Av in 1942, Hitler began his deportation of Jews from Warsaw to the death camps at Treblinka. Both the first and second temples were destroyed in Jerusalem on Tisha B'Av; with the destruction of the second temple, Jews were dispersed across the earth, and all the hideous atrocities that have since occurred to Jews can be traced to that one disastrous event. This midsummer date has seen the worst history can offer. That is why this story is entitled "Tisha B'Av."*

The hollow sound of night seeped through the screened windows. An occasional trashcan cover could be heard falling to the sidewalk with a frightening, reverberating, and shocking sound. An alley cat was having dinner. A ticking clock or a buzzing mosquito occasionally disturbed us, or the rumble of a single car passing swiftly through the night with an empty, lonely sound. The trees swished in the night breeze, singing their lullaby to the city. All was safe in our world. We were tucked in our beds, covered with cool white sheets. Our parents had said our night prayers. We always slept restlessly in the heat of the summer, but we slept more restlessly this night.

This is Uncle Oscar's story.

An unearthly howl cut through the night stillness. It was the broken voice of a man sobbing. It went on and on, wailing into a crescendo, its pathos spiraling up into the darkness. Mothers and fathers awakened, spoke in hushed, scared voices, and closed their windows to the hot night, but the sobbing, though muffled, could still be heard. I was aware of some of the fathers going downstairs and out into the night. I could hear struggling noises, the voices of the fathers, and the footsteps of many men. There was a tone and feeling in the air that I would later recognize, as an adult, as empathy, utmost care, and concern on the part of the fathers. The cries echoed and reverberated emptily like the sound of shouting into a tunnel. Finally, merciful sleep stilled the voice, and the night was quiet once more.

I lay there in the dark, wondering what had happened. My heart pounded with terror for what I did not understand. It had not been the voice of a ghost. It was real. I finally fell back to sleep, and in the morning, the night seemed a blurred memory of a bad dream.

I think we all faced the day groggily. My mother brought me to Auntie Dora's apartment in the morning so I could play with Leon in his bedroom while she and Auntie Dora sat in the kitchen. Leon and I thought that our mothers might talk about what had happened last night. We cracked open the bedroom door ever so slightly and crouched closely enough to listen to the story.

My mother spoke first. "Whatever happened to Oscar last night?"

Leon and I looked at each other with wide-eyed amazement, shocked that the voice had been Uncle Oscar's. Uncle Oscar—Neal and Yvette's father—was the voice in the night? It had been Uncle Oscar crying?

"*Yoi, yoi, yoi.*" Auntie Dora held her hand to her temple and closed her eyes, swaying back and forth. "You don't know what happened to Oscar?" she asked my mother in her Romanian accent. "I'm telling you…during the war, Oscar was sent to a death camp. One night some of the men were awakened and told to go to a certain place away from the camp. They were given shovels and forced to dig a huge hole in the ground. It took them a long time. When the ditch was deep enough, they were told by the guards to form a circle around the ditch. The guards shot them, one by one. Their bodies fell into the ditch. They had been digging their own grave. Oscar saw in a moment what was happening and jumped into the ditch before he could be shot, pretending to be dead. The bleeding bodies of his friends and even his brothers fell on top of him. More men fell in, again and again, until everyone who had been digging that hole had fallen in, dead. Oscar, terrified for his life, stayed a long time in the ditch. When he was certain that the guards had gone, he climbed out, covered with blood. He crawled on the ground like an animal and was able to escape from the death camp, but he was never the same. Every once in a while, he starts to remember what happened to him back then, and he loses his mind. His wife and family have a hard time when this happens to him." Auntie Dora sighed. "But life goes on, doesn't it? We have to make sure our children will never have to experience what we went through. You know, if you think about it, we didn't do anything. We were just Jews. It is always all right to hate us. That's how they were thinking."

Little did our mothers know that we, their two Jewish children, had been listening from behind the bedroom door, bewildered and frightened by what we had heard. The story and the sound of Uncle Oscar's terrified voice would stay with us for the rest of our lives. Our mothers didn't know it, but our identity was born in that moment. We were forever changed.

Scenes from Childhood

Alex in İsrael—Blind Man's Bluff

One hot day after another hit the east coast during the summer of 1954. Only one member of our little Jewish neighborhood was lucky enough to get a real vacation—Alex.

Alex lived in Auntie Dora and Uncle Louie's apartment. His entire family had perished in the Holocaust. He was in his early twenties, dashingly handsome, and an impeccable dresser, and he wore cologne. The other men in our community wore cologne only for special occasions, but Alex wore it every day. He had that Old World European charm and delightful accent. Leon and I teased him constantly. Leon even gave him the nickname of Schloima, a nonsense name, and it later became The Schloima, which was even worse.

Alex had decided it was time for him to find a bride and that he was going to Israel to accomplish this. This was no small thing in our neighborhood, where just going to the lake for a picnic was a big deal.

At the lake—in the background—for a picnic.

Everyone looked constantly for news from Alex, repeatedly asking each other, "So what's doing with Alex?" or "Any news from Alex yet?" The eagerly awaited news finally arrived in the form of a home movie and a letter from Alex. He had found his gorgeous Israeli bride! He was enclosing a film so that we, too, could see the wondrous sights of the Holy Land of our ancestors.

Auntie Dora hosted the momentous premiere of "Alex in Israel" in her apartment. She invited most of the neighborhood, and we joked that people were lining up for tickets. Her living room was turned into a small theater, with folding chairs arranged in straight rows. Uncle Louie set up the movie projector, and a white sheet was hung along one wall to serve as the movie screen. Borrowed fans kept the air moving. We children bathed early and arrived scrubbed and in our pajamas. Auntie Dora put out food for *nosh* and *schmooze* (snacks and conversation). This was the most exciting event of our summer!. We were fairly jiggling with anticipation.

Sometimes it's no easy task to quiet down a Jewish audience. We can be talkative and animated by nature—sometimes even the rabbi had to plead for silence in the *shul* (synagogue)—but not that night. Uncle Louie asked if we were ready to get started, and a silence fell immediately. Uncle Louie quipped, "Lights, camera, action!" And we were off to see the Holy Land, the land of our ancestors, Alex, and his new bride.

A Jewish movie audience seems to end up with a narrator in the crowd, especially back then when movie cameras did not record sound. The film began with what looked like a hotel room. Our narrator said, "See, he's starting us from the hotel so we can see where he is staying." Then Silah, Alex's new bride, came out from behind a closed door, smiled a beautiful smile, and waved to the camera. We all ooed and ahhed. The narrator said, "See, she's wearing a towel. Maybe they're going swimming and we'll get to see the Dead Sea."

Silah started to dance to music we couldn't hear, gyrating wildly and spinning around. Israeli music must be really lively! All of a sudden, she threw off her towel, and we all gasped in shock. She didn't have on a bathing suit. In fact, she didn't have any clothes on at all! Mothers scrambled in the dark, desperately grabbing their children and struggling to cover their eyes.

"Shut it off!" someone yelled. "Shut it off!"

Uncle Louie was struggling frantically, trying to find the switch to turn off the projector. Finally someone pulled the plug, and everything went dark. All we could hear was the filmstrip clacking around and around until coming at last to a stop. We sat in the dark, riveted with communal shock and disbelief. The silence lasted only for a moment.

The narrator found his voice. In an apologetic tone, almost a whisper, he said, "Alex sent the wrong movie."

I don't know who started it, but someone let out a nervous giggle, and soon everyone was laughing. Uncle Louie finally found the light switch, revealing an audience convulsed with uncontrollable laughter. Some were bending over holding their sides. Others had tears running down their cheeks. We children had never seen such unbridled glee.

Then, almost in unison, a quiet atmosphere extinguished the laughter, and everyone became serious. What to do?

Great discussions started, which is very typical of our people, and the men began to raise questions. Do we tell Alex? What will we do when he asks what we thought of his movie? How do we give it back to him to spare him embarrassment? And on it went for the rest of the summer. When Alex arrived home from Israel, he never asked about his movie, and Auntie Dora never told.

Scenes from Childhood

Coney Island and the Bath House

The dog days of summer were hard to bear anywhere, but they were especially hard to bear in the crowded, steaming, concrete city of Newark during the early 1950s. Parents offering a day trip to Coney Island caused sleepless nights of anticipatory excitement unparalleled by any other treat of childhood.

My mother began the preparation for our trip by packing bags of extra clothing and suntan oil. While she packed, she and my father dreamed aloud of walking the boardwalk in the late afternoon and eating a hot dog from Nathan's, a potato *knish*, and frozen custard. These were things to dream about when I was five years old. They talked of places and planned activities I would never forget: Steeplechase Park, Nathan's, The Cyclone, The Parachute Jump, The Carousel, and…the bath house?

Brother Allan on the Merry-Go-Round (carousel).

The trip to Coney Island involved a long ride on the subway. I can still remember the seats, uphol-stered with yellow wicker, woven just like a basket.

There were long benches and shorter benches for two people, oddly facing the opposite direction from the way the train was going. The worn spots on the woven wicker seats were edged with frayed fragments that stuck my legs like needles. The cars had overhead fans, and the fumes of diesel oil burned my eyes in a peculiar way. The lights on the train would go off every now and then, leaving us in noisy darkness while speeding through the black tunnel. This was an adventure far different from my everyday existence.

When we arrived at Coney Island at the Stillwell Avenue Station, it seemed there were hundreds of people pushing and clamoring to get to the beaches. The boardwalk aromas wafted a greeting of candy apples, cigar smoke, scrumptious hot dogs, and just a hint of the ocean.

How we actually got onto the beach is a blur to me now, lost in the deep recesses of my mind. It seems, though, that we went down sandy stairs from the boardwalk into an abyss called the ladies' locker room. It was smelly, hot, and dark, with wooden booths called lockers. In the background, the screams of riders on the Cyclone roller coaster above the bath house could be heard, along with the faint rat-tat-tat of the tracks on its wooden frame.

The dressing room doors of the bath house were wooden, too—crude, cracking, painted plywood worn with time. The cement floors were wet and slippery with runny gray sand. The stench of public toilets hung in the air, and the unbearable heat was ever present. We were each issued a metal tag with a number on it that hung on a rubberized bangle bracelet to be strapped around our ankles or wrists. It looked to me like a dog tag for a rabies license. A huge, unpleasant-looking woman in her fifties sat at a table in the oppressive heat, perfunctorily handing out beach tags. There was no smile, no "have a nice day" or "enjoy your visit". These were the days before corporate lessons in customer service were given for friendly communication.

We entered the beach from beneath the board-walk locker rooms. Under the boardwalk, the sand was strewn with sticks, bottles, papers, burnt ciga-rettes, and other trash, hurting my bare feet as I walked on them. There were people actually sitting on blankets in the dank darkness under the board-walk. Not us! We were bound for the sand and sun.

As we emerged from the dark underworld, we had to pause a moment to let our eyes adjust to the glaring sunlight. As far as the eye could see, human-ity stretched out on blankets, and beach umbrellas crowded the landscape. People struggled with heavy, wooden folding beach chairs canvassed in fabric striped with reds, blues, and greens. The sun beat down heavily on us, but there seemed mercifully to always be a breeze about, carrying the fragrance of suntan oil.

The ladies wore thick, black bathing suits with big skirts down to mid-thigh level and tight rubber bathing caps. Some men sported rented woolen bathing suits, which looked as unattractive to me as the ladies' suits. These ladies were not thin, fragile old ladies. They were the big-bosomed, top-heavy *bubbies* (grandmas) with leathery skin from years of summers in the sun.

There were ropes to hang onto in the water, planted deeply in the sand near the edge of the waves and stretching out towards the sea, where they were each attached to a floating barrel. I had no idea how the barrels stayed out there, but the ropes were big and strong. The ladies clung to them as if for dear life, dipping themselves up and down in the water, *kvelling*, "*Mechaya!*" (emoting expressions of bliss, like ooo and ahh and "what pleasure").

I built sandcastles and pail towers and searched for seashells along the shoreline with Mama. My father reclined like a Turkish king in his wooden beach chair. I thought he looked rather like an Arab sheik swathed in the bath towels he had piled on his head to keep his exceptionally white skin from burning. He entered the ocean only momentarily for a short swim, then took a cool shower, dressed, and went aloft to the boardwalk for the rest of the day to watch the sights. Wicker rickshaws that looked like huge baby buggies provided boardwalk transportation for "rich people" who didn't want to walk in the sun, but Papa didn't mind sitting alone on the boardwalk benches, and he happily occupied himself as a people watcher until the rest of us were ready to leave the beach.

We trudged back under the boardwalk and entered the same ladies' locker room, where our clothes were still hanging. My mother couldn't go to Coney Island without making a trip to the bath house. To this very day, I have no earthly idea why she thought this was a good thing. Apparently a lot of other women thought it was a good thing, too.

We had to pass once more by the unpleasant woman attending the locker room. We took a quick shower to rinse the sand from our bodies before being allowed to enter the steam room. What followed was something right out of Eastern Europe, Russia, and Poland.

We walked into a dark, steam-filled room so hot that I immediately began to choke and feared that I wouldn't be able to breathe. The old bubbies who had been hanging on to the ropes in the ocean were now in the steam room, only now they were completely naked. The hot fog of the steam was so thick that it was hard to see Mama just a few feet away. The bubbies were busy with pails of hot, soapy water and rags, slapping and beating themselves all over, all the while conversing loudly in Yiddish. Some were gasping loudly as they pulled a chain to cascade a bucketful of icy water down on them. I still couldn't breathe. My mother told me to bend down and breathe near the floor. The heat was gripping, and I was *shvitzing* (sweating) in panic. I screamed to my mother that I couldn't see, but no one noticed because they were too busy *schlepping* (dragging) their pails of hot soapy water along and delighting in the beautification treatment of the steam bath. Some women were even beating themselves with straw and something that looked like sprigs of herbal leaf bouquets. This was sheer torture for me.

Finally, after much begging and pleading not to have to do it, I submitted to the bucketful of freezing water splashing down on my head. I wrapped up in a towel while my mother slathered moisturizing lotion all over herself, again kvelling about the wondrous treatment and how it made her feel like "a million dollars." This is what people said back then if they felt really happy. To me, no one looked all that improved.

Coney Island – Stauch Baths

I couldn't wait to get up on the boardwalk and eat a hot dog from Nathan's, trimmed with what Papa called "the works." "The works" meant every-thing went on the hotdog— relish, mustard, ketch-up, and sauerkraut. Nathan's hot dogs were beef, but I doubt they were kosher. Apparently no one cared about that when it came to eating at Coney Island, not even Papa.

My parents always treated me to a few of the rides before we left to go back to Newark. My mother was described back then as a live wire, and she had actually ridden the famous Cyclone roller coaster alone, back in my parents' early dating days. Papa had been content to sit on a bench and read a newspaper while she rode her terrifying roller coaster. It had become a family story.

My father wasn't crazy about rides. I guess I got that from him. The large merry-go-round with its thousands of lights and calliope music made me sad for some reason. Instruments played on their own. The drum beat itself. The cymbals crashed together without human hands. The pipes on the calliope opened and closed eerily, surrounded by ornate paintings. There were carvings of strange topless angels, carved swirls, and men in togas playing long trumpets. The adornments looked creepy to me, as if they belonged to Mary the Syrian, the neighbor who told fortunes with her cards. I watched my jewel-studded steed moving up and down and looked at the crank on the ceiling, thinking that for sure my horse would somehow break off. The big chariots were painted in gaudy colors and gold, but they didn't look exciting because they didn't move like the horses did. I don't recall even one kid riding in one of them.

My father was not crazy about rides. I guess I got that from him.

It's funny—I know we came back, but I don't remember the trip home.

Scenes from Childhood

The Sukkah

Moishele told me his father was going to build a *sukkah* (a small hut topped with branches to mark the harvest holiday) in our backyard. I had no idea what he was talking about, but he was excited about it, so I was excited, too. Moishele and I were both five years old. I couldn't imagine anyone building something in our backyard. Our backyard was a huge, barren, flat expanse of cracked concrete shared by all six of the families who lived in the nearly one-hundred-year-old apartment building. The sun baked the oil-stained concrete. Overhead, six floors of clothesline ropes crossed the yard, with dancing sheets and colorful clothing flapping in the cool autumn breeze. The sheets looked like great billowing sails on a ship. When I looked at them I thought of Mr. Hammer, who threw fish heads out the window to feed the stray cats who were residents of this concrete field.

Overhead, six floors of clothesline ropes crossed the yard, with dancing sheets and colorful clothing flapping in the cool autumn breeze.

Moishele's father never smiled. I remember thinking that Moishele must be the whitest kid in the world. The sun bothered his eyes, and he always wore his *yarmulke*. I asked him one day if he wore it even when he took a bath. He laughed and skipped around in glee, but his father overheard my question and was clearly annoyed.

"What kind of a question is that?" he asked, turning and walking away from us. I felt bad that he was mad at me, but I didn't know what he meant. My question had been a wanting to know question. I didn't know yet that there was any other kind of question.

I told my parents about Moishele's *yarmulke* and about his father getting mad.

My mother frowned and said, "Why did you ask a question like that?"

My father said, "Moishele's father is a very religious man and our butcher. Don't ask silly questions."

It was right after the High Holy Days, and the weather was getting chilly, so we stayed inside. I noticed from the window that Moishele's father had dragged some large branches with leaves to the backyard, along with a pile of boards. I wondered what he was doing, but I didn't dare ask my parents another silly question. My father sounded excited though, just like Moishele. He said "Oh! It's *Succos*!"

He told me Moishele's father was probably building a sukkah. He said he would bring vegetables and fruits from his store and drop them off at Moishele's house. He and Uncle Eddie sometimes made pretty baskets of fruits for special occasions, and now I was wiggling with curiosity, but I didn't want to ask any more questions that seemed to annoy everyone.

And then there it was, right in our yard—a small shack with leafy tree branches for a roof. Moishele and his parents were all inside. His mother smiled at me and waved her hands for me to join them. When I stepped inside, I could hardly believe my eyes. There was an oriental carpet on the floor and pillows all around. It was cozy and warm, even though I could see the sky peeping through the leafy roof. There were braided garlic garlands from Papa hanging from the walls, apples in bushel baskets, and all sorts of fruits and vegetables. There was even a small barrel of pickles! This was a miracle. Moishele's mother looked like a queen as she sat on big pillows. Moishele's father took the *lulav*, which looked like a quiver of tree fronds. At the same time he held a funny little lemon called an *etrog* that he let me smell. It was a delightful bright yellow and smelled so good. He waved the fronds and lemon this way and that. Happiness was all around.

Moishele's mother told us that we were celebrating the harvest of the fields, giving thanks and remembering our poor Jewish houses. I didn't see the fields, and I had yet to understand our poor Jewish houses, but Moishele's father was smiling at me. I decided not to ask silly questions.

Sukkot is a weeklong festival during which religious Jews build a small hut in their backyards. The roof is made of branches and is open to the sky. This temporary shack, or sukkah, recreates the tents where Jewish farmers lived during the harvest. It also recalls the hastily made shelters during our many periods of exile.

Scenes from Childhood

The Neighborhood

For many of the residents, our neighborhood in Newark, New Jersey, had been the first place they called home after the Holocaust. First-generation American Jews lived there, as well—the sons and daughters of the Ashkenazi Jews who had come to America at the turn of the century. Small groups of *Hassidim* (Ultra-Orthodox Jews) and the gypsies made up another part of our working-class Jewish world.

Many American Jewish families experienced the loss of relatives through the Holocaust, and even though the sea and a full generation may have separated them, their loss was felt deeply. I once heard my father say that the entire *shtetl* (village) that my grandparents came from had been wiped off the face of the earth.

The tragic and cruel stories we heard in hushed voices were imprinted on our childhoods and identities forever. Regardless of where our modern-day wanderings would take us, the stories were always there and always would be.

Although our little neighborhood was in a declining, run-down section of Newark, it bustled with activities. It was the epitome of a place where the Old World met the New. The most important thing about it was that it was a happy place to be Jewish. Let me tell you about the people who dropped by almost daily in our bustling Jewish neighborhood in the 1950s.

There was the iceman, dressed in a leather apron. His brawny arms hauled blocks of dripping, melting ice off of his wet truck, leaving behind him a long trail of water as he *schlepped* the block of ice upstairs to tenants who had iceboxes. (Not everyone had a refrigerator, and those who did called them Frigidaires regardless of the manufacturer.) They were made of solid oak and porcelain. The pantries in the building had central drains in the floor to allow the melted ice a direct line to the sewer.

There was a seltzer man who delivered little bottles of seltzer in heavy wooden boxes. The bottles had charges on them to produce the carbon dioxide. We children were told not to touch the charges because they were bombs. Who knew?

There was the milkman, who came in his white uniform to our back door every couple of days to slip glass bottles of milk into an insulated aluminum box outside our door. The milkman was jokingly rumored to be the father of any kid in the neighborhood who didn't look like his natural father.

The umbrella man wandered in and out of our neighborhood in a long, black coat and a broad-brimmed black hat. He looked shifty-eyed and sneaky, his beady little black eyes darting nervously this way and that. He carried a knife-sharpening contraption on his back with a wheel that spun around, and he assured all the Jewish customers that it was kosher. He fixed leaky umbrellas, too—umbrellas that had their ribs pulled loose from being blown inside out too many times. I wondered how a man could make a living from sharpening knives and fixing umbrellas.

There was an egg boy who delivered kosher eggs to the neighborhood. He rode a bicycle with a large basket attached to the front handlebars to hold the eggs. It would have been a tragedy had he ever fallen off his bicycle. It would've been doubly tragic for my family, because my brother was the egg boy. He had the important-sounding job of candler for the rabbi. He would sit in a small, dark, dungeon-like room and hold each and every egg up to a light bulb that dangled from an electric cord in the ceiling, to make certain that there was no flaw in the egg. Kosher eggs can never have a spot of blood in them or be fertilized, as that would render them *treif* (unfit). The flawed eggs were discarded. The good eggs were approved, the rabbi prayed the egg blessing over them, and Allan, my brother, delivered the eggs. It was a good job for a high school boy. He later became an engineer.

We were not without strange characters in our midst. Mr. Hammer made great gefilte fish, but it was rumored that he kept his carp fish swimming around in his bathtub. Mrs. Rosen forced Mr. Rosen to live in the garage.

The egg boy – my brother Allan.

Moishele's father, Simon, had a live butcher shop with sheep and chickens in little pens and lots of sawdust on the floor. Auntie Dora bought fresh meat from Simon for every *Shabbos* (Sabbath). Leon and I enjoyed the butcher shop; it was a sort of Jewish petting zoo.

On Sunday afternoons, a pony man came to the neighborhood offering rides through the neighborhood on his pony.

The pony man offered rides for the neighborhood kids.

The Fuller Brush man might knock on the door, or the insurance salesman collecting his weekly premiums, or even the dreaded vacuum salesman who would throw dirt all over the carpet to show how great his vacuum worked. The women of the neighborhood had a calling chain set up to alert each other that these salesmen were in the neighborhood so that everyone knew when not to answer the door unless they really wanted brushes or a new vacuum.

Our apartment homes were heated with hard, shiny anthracite coal, and huge coal trucks arrived noisily each fall, a sign that autumn and winter would soon be coming. The heavy trucks rumbled into our neighborhood bearing strange names like Lackawanna Coal Company and N.E. Penn. Papa paid twenty-six dollars for a ton of coal to heat our apartment for a month. The coal was transferred into our cellar by long chutes that resembled sliding boards at the park. These chutes hooked onto the truck and fitted through cellar windows. Amidst the shouts of the coal-men giving orders, the huge dump truck slowly cranked its bed up until it was pointing to the sky, spilling the ton of coal into the chute and down into a scary room called the coal bin. Some people didn't have windows to their coal bins, and the black men had to toil up and down cellar stairs, carrying 100-pound bags of coal on their backs. The bags were made of thick, rough hemp cloth with straps for carrying, and the men had to make many trips down to the coal bins, up to the street to refill the sacks, and back down to the bins, again and again. It was exhausting, filthy work. The men and their clothes were covered in black coal dust.

Papa and Mama shared the chore of going down three flights of stairs to shovel coal into our cellar furnace a few times each day. The coal stood like a great pyramid of rocks stored in the dark, locked coal bin. Mornings would bring the chore of shaking down the ashes and shoveling them into huge pails that had to be carried upstairs and put out on the street with the trash. Those buckets full of ashes weighed a lot. When it snowed, the ashes were strewn over the sidewalks to create friction to keep people from falling on the ice.

Papa always threw a shovel of coal into the furnace in the morning before leaving for work. The heat hissed and clanked in the steam pipes, releasing comforting warmth in our childhood mornings. I felt loved by Papa when he did this every morning, although I don't think he ever actually told me he loved me.

Scenes from Childhood

Daily Life—Cilia Visits

We owned one radio, and it was turned on the moment my mother came into the kitchen in the morning. That radio and the smell of coffee meant Mama was up. We listened to songs like "Jezebel" by Frankie Laine. My brother Allan loved that song. It might have been one of my earliest Bible lessons. Big brothers like to scare their little sisters with gory stories, and Jezebel was a perfect one for that. Dogs devoured Jezebel because of her wickedness—ewww! Then there was Rosemary Clooney belting out "Mambo Italiano," and my favorite, "Daddy Dear Tell Me Please." Leon and I knew all the words to Fess Parker's "Ballad of Davy Crockett."

Oilcloth graced our kitchen tables. Pictures of Borden's Elsie the Cow must have been given out free somewhere, because everyone seemed to have her picture on their wall. Our stove had a *blech* (a metal cover for the top of the stove). My mother used to heat it up on our gas stove. When Shabbos came and the lights went out and the stoves went off, the blech continued to keep our food hot. I was burned on it quite a few times. We had two battleship gray washtubs in our kitchen for laundering clothes. The hot water heater was out in the open, sitting in a corner of the kitchen. Papa liked to lean his back on it when he got home from work.

My brother took woodshop class in school. Only boys could take that class. They had to make a cutting board in the shape of a pig whose squiggly little tail had a hole in it so it could be hung on the wall. Mama never used the one my brother made, but it hung in our kitchen as a proud decoration for years. It became a neighborhood joke that the Ottensteins had a pig in their kitchen, but so did a bunch of other Jewish people. Folks in the neighborhood wondered why there wasn't some other shape for a cutting board. "There must be," people would say. "There must be another choice." I guess there wasn't, because they were still making pig-shaped cutting boards when I went to school years later.

We could count on visitors coming to our doors just as frequently as vendors and delivery-men. Sometimes they came to have a cup of coffee. Sometimes my father's brothers, Uncle Bernie or Uncle Davy, would pop in for lunch. Mary the Syrian came to tell fortunes. Then there was mean Mrs. Rosen, our landlady, who was always looking for our rent. Once she shouted that she would throw a bucket of hot water out the window on us children if we didn't get away from her window. Our mothers overheard her say it, and they began fighting with her from their windows, yelling at her even though she was the landlady. I don't know what became of the issue, but my mother told me later, "Just stay away from Mrs. Rosen's window, please. She's an old woman."

One time Mama gave all of our food to a woman who came to our door and claimed to be a poor widow with no food for her children. Mama told Auntie Dora about it on the telephone.

"*Yoi*, Joan, I gave her all my food, too!" Auntie Dora moaned.

"But Dora, I gave her lots of clothes, too."

"You did? *Na* [Aha]! I'm telling you, I did, too."

The two women laughed about it for years, because they saw the same woman the next day, making her rounds at the other apartments. "How could she have eaten all that food so fast?" they joked. "How could she schlep all of that down the street? She must have had a get-away car!" The husbands were not happy with the story.

"She saw you coming," Papa said.

Another frequent visitor we could count on was Celia Mitdabristen. Not only was Celia known as the neighborhood *yenta* (gossiper), she was also famous for something else that I didn't know about at the time.

One day during Chanukah time, my mother was peeling potatoes for *latkes* (potato pancakes). Several other neighborhood women were chopping onions around our kitchen table. There came a knock on the door. Mama told me to go to the door to see who was there. When I opened the door, Celia was standing there.

"Who's at the door?" Mama called to me.

"It's Celia," I called back. "Celia Mitdabristen."

There was dead silence from the kitchen. Then I heard someone breathe an *oiy*. Celia pushed by me impatiently and let herself into the kitchen. With her hands on her hips, she looked around at the other women at the table.

"So," she said, "it's Celia mit da Bristen, eh? Very nice, very nice. So that's what you're saying about Celia when she's not here. Move over and give me a potato. I'll peel."

That was the day I learned that Mitdabristen was not a surname; *mit da Bristen* is Yiddish for "with the breasts."

Scenes from Childhood

The Vegetable Man

" "Tomatoes, tomatoes! Fresh ripe tomatoes!" called the vegetable man. Even before I heard his calls, I knew he was in the neighborhood by the clip-clop of his horse's hooves on the red cobblestone street. I looked out from our sun parlor windows to see his big brown horse and huge, weatherworn wagon three floors below me. The horse had blinders on his eyes. Mama said the blinders were so that the poor animal wouldn't see the cars and get scared. I liked the vegetable man, because when the mothers came out to buy fruit and vegetables from him, we children got to pet his horse and visit with our friends.

The driver of the wagon was a short, swarthy, squinty-eyed man with leather-like skin, known only as the vegetable man. He always wore a cap, an apron, and a serious face. His large wagon was filled with produce arranged in neat sections. There were brown paper bags and a dangling scale that swung back and forth, clanking as the horse trudged obediently along.

I don't know why, but even if his fruit looked perfect, the other mothers found something wrong with it. He would say things like "beautiful," "sweet as sugar," and "fresh," but the women always argued with him until he'd end up putting one more potato or some extra apples in their bags. After all the noise and haggling, the ladies went away happy enough.

My mother always seemed annoyed with the other women for haggling. She said that the man had enough trouble trying to earn a living and that it was degrading to try to make him sell everything cheaper. We ourselves had no need to buy anything from him because Papa and Uncle Eddie had a produce store, but Mama would buy a little something each time he came. Perhaps she did it just because I wanted to see the horse, or maybe she felt sorry for the man. That's the way my mother was.

Looking down from our window, I saw the vegetable man park his wagon down the street under the shade of a large old maple tree near the shoemaker. He hung a huge canvas bucket filled with oats around his old horse's neck and patted the animal gently. As I watched, he pulled himself back up onto the wagon, using a handle mounted on the side of the wagon. He sat high on the wooden bench behind his hardworking friend. The vegetable man and his horse had their lunch together in the quiet shade of the old maple. Even a child wondered where the vegetable man lived.

Scenes from Childhood

The Concert

The windows facing out onto our concrete backyard were usually opened wide in the early part of the morning, even in the winter. My mother said it was to air out the house, but I used to wonder. Straining my eyes upward in the sunlight, I could see that each and every open window in the entire building had a feather-down quilt stuffed into it. This was a morning ritual—airing the bedclothes on a nice day, turning them every now and then to make sure each side caught the hot sun. My mother said it was to refresh them and kill the germs.

Some days the windows were open for a better reason, or at least one that I appreciated a lot more. My mother had to hold me tightly in the open window on those special days, so I could lean over the windowsill to get a good look at what was about to happen three floors below. The oil-stained concrete expanse that was our backyard became a merry stage. The accordion man had arrived! Women wearing *babushkas* (headscarves) called to each other from their windows to make sure everyone knew. Although the women came from several different countries, all of them could speak Yiddish, even if just a *bisel* (little), and they knew the same songs.

It was no matter that the ladies wore headscarves instead of diamond tiaras; our open windows had transformed into box seats at the opera. They called down their tunes for him to sing and play on his accordion. He had a little monkey tied to him with a chain who held out a dented tin cup for tips. I liked the monkey more than the music.

Our backyard three floors below.

Our fathers were always at work when the accordion man came. Maybe they didn't even know about the accordion man and his once-in-a-while morning serenades. It was a great treat for us. The mothers mocked each other lightheartedly for their selections of old world tunes—tunes I never heard on the radio, but tunes I would never forget. I remember the jingling little pings of sound as the women happily tossed down coins that landed lightly on the cracked pavement. I could see on some of their out-stretched arms the tattooed numbers of the camps. Could some of them have been the same Jewish women who had stretched out their arms when the camps were liberated? These were the post war mothers—mothers of the Holocaust, but also mothers in a happier place and a happier time.

The little monkey scurried about, picking up the coins and placing them in his dented tin cup. The accordion man removed his battered hat, stretched out his arms in a great gesture of appreciation, and bowed low, hugging his hat to his heart. We applauded him delightedly from our box seats, and then the women closed the windows. Before my mother closed our window, I saw the little monkey climb onto the accordion man's arm and up onto his shoulder. They shuffled away. Even a child like me wondered where the accordion man lived.

Frightening Stories

The Exodus

F orests capture our imaginations. They figure in our childhood bedtime stories, such as "Hansel and Gretel" and "Goldilocks and the Three Bears." The forest is at once magnificent and foreboding, dark and deep, full of shadows and whispers and cries. Yes, cries.

Under the stars, under the towering pines, without shelter, we stayed like animals in a field. The rain fell on the sick, the old, and the young. Drenched and shivering, our clothes eventually dried. When the leaves pulled backward against the wind and high above our heads the trees twisted and danced in ominous fury, we knew this was the warn-

*ing that rain would come. Nature kept her cruel promise,
and rain it did.*

*Even a cow has a barn, and even a horse a stable, but
we were not worth a roof for our heads. The mud became
our beds and the rain our blankets, for we were the Jews.*

Every year at our Passover *seders* (the Passover
meal served with the story of the exodus), we are
asked to become slaves again. We are asked to follow
Moses into the wilderness and wander across barren
lands. G-d opened the sea, and we crossed over it
to freedom, fleeing from those who sought our use
and destruction.

No one ever asked us to imagine leaving our
homes in the humble *shtetls*. No one asked us to
imagine how in such haste there was little opportunity to feel the iron door that slammed shut on what
had been our lives. No parent told us to imagine
how it felt to leave our pets, toys, and treasured objects. Did we stand with our parents at our gates in a
trance-like state, waiting to be led like animals to an
unknown fate? Yes, we stood there.

We walked for three hours along the familiar
roads—the young, the old, and the afflicted. We saw
our Christian neighbors looking at us as we trudged
along. I wondered what they thought. Were we not
the same children who were invited sometimes into

their homes to take a candy treat off the Christmas tree?

I can remember the springtime, because Auntie Dora told me it was springtime, and I was there. It was springtime because it was just after the Jewish holiday of Shavuot. How ironic for us, the Jews. Shavuot marks an event so important that it changed the world—our world; it was the giving of the five books of Moses, the Torah—the Torah, with the Ten Commandments, the very instructions from G-d for human dignity and behavior. What happened to mankind on this day? Some wondered silently where was our G-d.

We arrived at the edge of the forest of Bungur, our ghetto. I slept on the ground with Auntie Dora and ate the melting snow. I was there when the rain poured down on us. All we could do was sit there and wait. We sat *shiva* (mourning time) for ourselves, but there was no one to say, "May heaven comfort you."

Frightening Stories

A Love Story

I had spent the night at the Rosenfeld's apartment. Just like kids today, sleeping at a friend's house was an event and treat much looked forward to. In the morning Leon was off somewhere in another room playing with "boys' toys." I was still in the bedroom helping Auntie Dora make the bed with a luxurious bedspread made of silky golden damask. I always thought of Auntie Dora as a fancy lady. She wore delicate jewelry and lovely clothes, and her home reflected the same appreciation of good quality, grace, and elegance.

We finished making the bed, and I wandered over to her dresser to study her perfume bottles. They were cut crystal glass in shades of blue, topaz, and rose, with little rubber bulb atomizers on them. Auntie Dora saw me looking admiringly at them and teasingly picked one up and squirted me with its incredibly wonderful fragrance.

Also on her dresser was an ornate comb, brush, and hand mirror that looked like they could have belonged to a queen. They were fashioned from tortoiseshell and mother of pearl. Auntie Dora brushed my hair with the regal brush and told me she hoped that someday she would have a little girl, too. She told me she would name her daughter Elizabeth, after her mother.

Auntie Dora smiled wistfully as she opened one of the dresser drawers and took out a delicate scarf with pale flowers stitched in golden thread. She wrapped it gently about my face and shoulders and cupped my face in her hands. She told me I was such a *shane madele* (beautiful girl). She started singing a melody from her country. Later in my life, I would remember it and learn that it was the Hungarian Czardas. She spun me around and around as I held on to her finger. We sat down at the foot of the bed.

Auntie Dora looked thoughtfully at me. "Did you know that I used to live in a place called Transylvania when I was a young girl?" she asked. She didn't wait for me to answer. "We lived in a nice house. The neighborhood was not like this." I suddenly felt she disliked our neighborhood because she wrinkled up her nose, and I listened closely. "My sisters and I would go dancing and had pretty dresses. We had a happy life. That was all before Hitler came, and the war."

Curiosity and innocence spurred me to ask Auntie Dora where her sisters and mama were. She looked out the sunny bedroom window, and I saw her face change. She didn't answer me. She wiped tears from her eyes with the delicate scarf I had just been wearing for our dance. When I got home, I asked Mama about Auntie Dora's family, and Mama told me the following story.

Frightening Stories

A Child's First
Holocaust Story

Mama told me Hitler was a terrible man who forced all the Jews to leave their houses in Transylvania. "Auntie Dora's pets, her toys—everything was left behind," Mama said. "She was about thirteen years old. Auntie Dora and all the other Jewish neighbors who lived in her city, Dej, had to walk for hours and hours along the roads to get to a forest called Bungur. She, her family, and all the families she knew lived in that forest for a long time. She said it was freezing there and scary. They stayed there, even in the rain, and lived there for several months.

"One day the cruel men forced everyone to walk to a train station far, far away from the forest. They had to ride a horrid train stuffed with all sorts of people, all being taken away to work. She said that after her family and neighbors arrived in the work camp, other Jewish people who had been there for a long time began to beat them, scratch them, and slap them. They were screaming at the newcomers out of resentment that they had had more time to enjoy their lives while their fellow Jews were suffering. Do you understand how much badness there was at that time?"

Mama continued, "Your Auntie Dora was forced to take a shower in freezing water, and a woman shaved off all her hair. She didn't even recognize her own sisters without their hair. Then they had to form two lines; the line on the right was for mamas without young children. Auntie Dora was in that line with her mother, because her brother and three sisters were not little children. It was bitter cold, and an icy wind was blowing. A lady in the left line was shivering and struggling with her small children. Auntie Dora's mother gave the lady a sweater and held the hand of one of her children while the lady tried to get the rest of the children together.

Along came a mean guard who shouted at Auntie Dora's mother because she was in the wrong line. He pushed her into the line of women with young children. She tried to tell him that the child was not her child and that she was only helping the lady with her children. She was so scared of going in that the left line; she wanted to stay with Auntie Dora. She wailed and told the man over and over again, 'This child is not mine!'

"It was no use. It was hopeless. Auntie Dora's brother Leopold ended up getting pushed into the left line with their mama, and he wasn't even a Bar Mitzvah yet. I think he was a tall boy of twelve. Sadly, Auntie Dora's mama, the other mamas, and their children walked away. Auntie Dora's mother turned around and said to Auntie Dora and her sisters, 'Take care of yourselves and stay together.' Auntie Dora never saw her mother and brother again."

I asked Mama why the guards had taken Auntie Dora's mother and her brother. Mama looked at first like she wasn't going to tell me. She looked like she felt she had told me too much of the story already. So I asked again, "Mama, why did those men take Auntie Dora's mother and brother away?"

"Auntie Dora's mother and brother were killed," Mama said finally. "They were killed because…because they were Jewish."

I sat still for a minute, thinking about her answer and how scared she looked after she said it. Her answer seemed outrageous, but a little child doesn't know the word outrageous. I just knew the answer had to be impossible.

"Mama," I said finally, "Auntie Dora is Jewish, too."

"Yes," Mama answered, "but she and her sisters could still work hard. Little children and old mothers were useless in the work camps. Anyone who was sick or old or too young was…was… killed."

This was a terrible story. My poor Auntie Dora! I remembered how she had wiped her tear away with the beautiful scarf that very morning.

"Your Auntie Dora was blessed with Leon," Mama said. "Who knows? Someday maybe she will have a daughter—a beautiful daughter just like you. You know, she told me that she would name her daughter Elizabeth after her mama. And do you know what? Her own mama's wish came true. Auntie Dora's sisters—Eva, Magda, and Erna—stayed together. And together they left the terrible place called Auschwitz."

The experiences of the Holocaust were always present just below the emotional surface of many of the people I knew at this tender age. Just as in this story, life's happy moments could change in the blink of an eye from times of joy to tormenting memories of a tragic past.

Dora did have a baby girl when Leon and I were about ten years old. She named her Elizabeth.

Dora Rosenfeld, Leon Rosenfeld, and me. High Holy Days c. 1954.

Frightening Stories

The Cage—Pleading Child

In Auschwitz the showers for bathing were on a small hill. Those showers were some distance away from the big yard, across from the warehouse block, where Auntie Dora sorted piles of clothes on tables. She would soon learn that there was another kind of shower. She was thirteen years old.

One day when Auntie Dora went up the hill to shower, a girl whispered to her, "You see that black smoke over there? It's burning night and day. What do you think that is, stupid girl? You don't know that there is another kind of shower? People go there and don't come out alive! People from the shower are being burned up over there. Your parents burned up over there, and other people who couldn't work as hard as us. You will see. After you can't work any-more, when you're too sick and tired, they'll come and take you away, too, to kill you and burn you up."

When Auntie Dora told me the story, I wondered how such a thing could be true. Surely the girl had just wanted to scare Auntie Dora. But Auntie Dora told me that after what the girl had said, she looked at those smoke stacks more closely and wondered.

~ ~ ~

On another day when Auntie Dora went to the showers, she saw a cage in the middle of the com-pound, almost like a dog kennel. She went over to the cage and saw a girl she knew from her school inside.

"What are you doing in there?" she asked the girl.

"I don't know. They just came and got me and put me in here."

"*Na!*" Auntie Dora gasped. "What are you going to do?"

The girl shrugged her shoulders. "Dora, what *can* I do?"

It was still springtime, and the air was warm. Auntie Dora saw the girl in the cage every day, out in the open for everyone to see.

"I guess they came and gave her food, but the cage had no roof," Auntie Dora told me. "It was a sort of pen. When it rained, she just sat there, getting wet. The summer came, and she was still in the cage, with the sun hot and shining on her. Of course, it got colder and colder as fall came, and she still had the same clothes on as when I first saw her there.

"'What will happen to me, Dora?' the girl called out to me one day. 'Soon it will start to snow, and then what? I'm already freezing in here!'

"Think about it, Harriet. Nobody could do anything. Just think how it was for everybody to see a girl like that, freezing in the falling snow, trying to keep warm out there. She was rolled up into a tiny, shivering ball. I was cold already with only a thin blanket on my wooden bed. We hardly ever went to the showers because of the snow, and because we couldn't bear to see the girl in the cage.

"When the snow melted, the cage wasn't there anymore, and my friend was gone. It seemed that G-d had forgotten us."

From Strange Lands

The Dream

When I was a little girl, Papa and I visited Bubby Zelda almost every Sunday. She lived alone in the public housing near the old surrey horse-racing track in Newark's Weequahic Park. The visits were always fun for me because not only did I get to see my bubby, who always had cookies baked and ready, but I also got to visit the stables across the street from her apartment.

There were not just horses in those stables; chickens and goats ran around the grounds, as well. Papa said it was because the horses needed company and ran better if they weren't lonely. He would bring sugar cubes, carrots, and cut apples to give the horses, and he showed me how to hold my hand out flat so the horses could nibble the sugar from my palm without nibbling my hand. Papa knew a lot about horses. He told me about a horse he had once owned named Charlie. Charlie was a white horse, and Papa took pride in keeping him as white as the snow. Charlie pulled the huge wagon my grandfather used for selling vegetables and fruits through the streets of Newark.

Those Sundays were special days with Papa. After visiting Bubby, we'd eat at the Weequahic Diner, which was famous for its great Jewish food. Papa let me put coins in the jukebox and choose any song I wanted, and he'd ask me why I liked the songs I chose.

My grandmother came to America about 1904, at the age of sixteen. She paid fifty dollars for her steerage ticket across the ocean from her little village in Russia called *Jashunovka* (Jasienowka), which was about twelve kilometers from Bialystok. What did Bubby want in America? What was her dream?

Here is my grandmother's dream, as told to me as a child in her thick Yiddish accent.

"Jashunovka had a population of about one hundred families. If you want to get an idea of what the *shtetl* looked like, imagine the stories of Sholem Aleichem. We lived in a wooden house with only two rooms. There was a huge oven in the kitchen. The floors were all yellow pine wood, and my mother kept them spotlessly clean. The winters were freezing. Do you know that the snow came up over the doors of the houses? My father had to dig a tunnel for us to open our door.

"All seven of us children slept in the same bedroom as our parents, on pillows and beds made from goose down. We had only about a tablespoonful of meat once a week on Shabbos. We ate mostly bread, barley, beans, cabbage, beets, onions, pickles, milk, eggs, and potatoes. At Chanukah time, we were treated with oranges imported from Palestine. They tasted like heaven.

"We took only one weekly bath at the public bathhouse, as well as our *mikveh* (Jewish ritual bath). My mother, may she rest in peace, used to braid our hair in one long braid hanging down our backs. She made all our dresses from gingham cloth, a different color for each of us. We always put on clean clothes for *Shabbos*.

"Our fathers and brothers worked in the tannery, making coats of sheepskin for both the Jews and Russians who lived in our town. They went from house to house taking the measurements of the townspeople. One of your great-grandfathers, however, was an artist; he did the woodcarving for the shul. He carved out a beautiful tree with the history of the Ottenstein family. It's in a synagogue somewhere here in New Jersey. The family should have kept it," Bubby fussed. "Now it's just a decoration.

"The Poles and Russians in Jashunovka separated themselves from us, of course, and in return we kept ourselves from them as much as possible. We were lucky, because we did not have any *pogroms* (attacks on Jews) in our town. Only our men learned how to speak Russian and Polish. We girls and women only knew how to speak Yiddish. The Jewish newspaper was printed in Yiddish. Men learned to read Hebrew so they could read prayers. (Yiddish is written using Hebrew letters, but comes out sounding like a Germanic language). The men were also taught to sound out words and could write Polish and Russian or any other language this way. Our men were literate before any of the peasants had ever learned to read and write. Unfortunately, we women weren't given a chance to learn to read.

"As soon as I got to America, I was looking for a teacher who could teach me how to read and write in both Yiddish and English, and how to pray. I got a

job cooking in a restaurant. That restaurant later became the automat—you know, the restaurants where
you see sandwiches and pies in glass cabinets. People
inserted coins in a slot and then they could open the
little door to get a meal—an American invention."
Bubby laughed gleefully as she remembered it.

"My language teacher came to the house a few
times a week, and I would pay him out of my earn-
ings at the restaurant. I learned what I wanted to
learn. Little by little, I saved my money, but I always
bought a banana every day. I thought the banana
was the most wonderful fruit in the world.

"So what do you think I wanted more of in
America? Turn around and look. You see that sec-
retary desk? I saved every penny to get that desk for
myself. I wanted to put books in it; books that I could
say I had read. I wanted to be able to open it up and
write with a pen and ink. When I die, from all my
grandchildren, I am giving that desk to you. Why?
You are interested in Jashunovka and Jewish life and
how things were. I see you writing down all the time
what I tell you. You deserve to keep my dream."

From Strange Lands and People

A Curious Story

Auntie Dora and Uncle Louie always had houseguests or temporary boarders staying in their small apartment. The guests were always survivors of the Holocaust. Two of the guests who passed through their home were Mr. Frankel and his aged father.

I remember Mr. Frankel as a tall, blond young man. His blue eyes were sad and sensitive, and he spoke with a delightful Polish accent. I learned I could make his sad eyes smile with my songs and dances and silly pranks; he would stare at me across

Auntie Dora's table and wink at me. But his father was another story altogether.

To my young eyes, the elderly Mr. Frankel was the skinniest man in the whole wide world. He was also the whitest, holiest, and most serious man I could imagine. He probably was the loneliest man, as well.

You see, old Mr. Frankel had lost everything in the Holocaust, including his wife and all his children, except for the young Mr. Frankel. My mother warned us that he could not tolerate noisy children because of all his horrible memories. Indeed, Leon and I annoyed him just by being present. Our playing clearly irritated him. Auntie Dora and Uncle Louie had great respect for him, however, and they tried to make him comfortable.

Old Mr. Frankel stayed alone in his bedroom all day, the door cracked open just a bit. Despite firm instructions to stay away, I often peeked in through the door, always finding him near the window, straining to see the pages of his prayer book by the sunlight. I can still picture him there now. Occasionally he would raise his eyes to heaven and then close them so tightly that his face twisted in what I now know was agony.

One hot day in the city summer, Auntie Dora, Uncle Louie, and my parents decided to take a picnic lunch to the lake in the country. Leon and I were ecstatic at the chance to get out of the city and jump into the lake. Auntie Dora and Mama began preparing our favorite picnic foods, deciding to make it a dairy meal. Because Jews cannot eat both milk and meat in the same meal, a dairy meal meant that we would have tuna salad sandwiches and hardboiled eggs, which are *pareve* (neutral), considered neither meat nor milk. Auntie Dora and Mama also packed macaroni salad, potato salad, coleslaw, and a wonderful, cold pink soup called *borscht*, made from beets, which was served with great dollops of sour cream. Cantaloupes, grapes, watermelon, or fresh peaches went along, as well, and no picnic would be complete without Heinz vegetarian beans and, of course, fresh kosher pickles. On the way home, we'd stop at a dairy farm that sold homemade ice cream.

Leon and I were sent to the corner grocery store to get the pickles. In those days, pickles in the store floated in open barrels of heavenly brine and were fished out with tongs. The grocery man wrapped them in white paper and handed us the delicious-smelling package.

My parents, Auntie Dora, and Uncle Louie invited the younger Mr. Frankel to come with us on the outing. It took some coaxing, but Leon and I were thrilled when he was finally convinced to join us. He brought his camera, an old box camera from Europe that he had managed to bring to America with him after the war. He liked to develop his own pictures in a darkroom with tubs of magical water. We thought it was amazing.

Many years later, when I was a first-year piano major at the Manhattan School of Music in New York City, I commuted each day to New York from New Jersey. What a schlep! I had decided to take on some beginning piano students of my own, and as I developed relationships with the families of my little prodigies, I realized that three of my pupils had parents who were survivors of the Holocaust. This was not a surprise, because almost all of us had moved a town or two away from the crumbling city of Newark in a steady exodus to Irvington or Maplewood, migrants moving up the hill en masse, both literally and figuratively.

Sometime in December, during the holiday vacation, I made plans to have a piano recital in my parents' living room. It would be a "salon" recital, cozy and intimate, with good Jewish food and *nachas* (joy, good feeling). The father of one of my students brought his old camera to the recital. His wife was annoyed and warned that the camera had film in it from ages ago and probably would not take any pictures. The man said he just wanted to experiment and see what was on the original roll of film. He was planning to develop it himself.

"So he has to experiment tonight," his wife groaned to us. "The camera has been on the closet shelf for *years*. Okay, okay," she sighed, "but take some photos with the new camera, too, so that at least we'll have our daughter's first recital recorded." This sort of bantering is very Jewish, and it is not in the least hostile. We all took it in stride and waited for the little skirmish to end so the recital could begin.

The recital was a big success, and I thought no more about the old camera.

A week after the recital, my student's father came with his daughter for her piano lesson, instead of her mother, who usually was the one who accompanied her. The man was almost shaking with excitement. Out of neat envelopes, he produced the recital photos, all in black and white. Then, with trembling hands, he withdrew another photo from the large envelope, keeping it facing towards himself.

"Miss Ottenstein, I have a question for you," he said, his voice unsteady with emotion. "When I was developing the photos from my old camera—you know, the one my wife didn't want me to use—there in the dark room I saw the face of a little girl on the same film. I said to myself, 'I know this face. I *know* this face.'" He took a breath and turned the photo so I could see it. "Is this you? Is this little dancing girl from a picnic at a lake *you?*"

"Is this you? Is this little dancing girl from a picnic at a lake you?"

I could not believe my eyes. Yes, indeed, it *was* me! My image had stayed in that camera for almost fifteen years, emerging uncannily on the same film as photos of me as an adult. I was still connected to Mr. Frankel, and I'd had no idea that my little student was the daughter of the Mr. Frankel of my childhood.

Yes, indeed, it was me!

Mr. Frankel had been busy working during scheduled piano lessons and had not had the opportunity to see my parents, which is why he never realized that my parents and I were his neighbors. We had been a part of his first days in America, of his humble beginnings in Auntie Dora's apartment, and of one bright summer day when life for him—out from under the shadow of the Holocaust—could almost look good again.

> *Why the separation of meat and milk? Why was the picnic "dairy"?*
>> *The first of the first fruits of thy ground thou shalt bring to the house of haShem thy G-d; thou shalt not seethe [boil] a kid in its mother's milk. (Exodus 23:19)*
> *This means there is no lasagna, chicken Alfredo, or cheeseburgers for us. Plates or dishes used to prepare meat must be kept apart from dishes used for dairy products. Even the pots, pans, and cutting boards are separated. There are two bars of kosher soap and two sinks. Meat and milk products cannot be placed on the same table, and observant Jews wait at least four hours after consuming meat before eating dairy. Are these rules hard to follow? Yes. Sometimes the rules serve the purpose of reminding us of G-d with each bite of food. We are following the Torah, G-d's Law. Eating becomes a religious act.*

From Strange Lands and People

The Samovar

He stood like a proud sentinel on his crocheted doily, the focal point of a slim, ornate table. The mysterious markings carved in his burnished brass were subtle evidence that he was better than all the rest of the possessions found in this modest dwelling. Charcoal burned at his base. He was the samovar. Even his name—Samovar—rang with an exotic melody. As children, we sensed the samovar came from far away in a strange land and from another time, but this proud prince's abode was now the lowly basement-level apartment of Bubby Marcus.

Even his name—Samovar—rang with an exotic melody.

Bubby Marcus was not really my bubby. She was the neighborhood bubby, a bubby to all children who no longer had a bubby. There were too many of those children in our neighborhood, living without their grandparents because of places with names like Auschwitz, Bergen-Belsen, and Dachau.

Bubby Marcus had brought her prized samovar—the symbol of Russian hospitality—from her far-off home in Russia, my mother explained. The samovar was used for making tea. As such, it was a very useful Shabbos item for us. The charcoal at its base and center pipe were ignited before sunset, since it is forbidden for Jews to light fires after sundown when the Sabbath begins. We are commanded by G-d to rest, and making a fire is considered work, as it was back in biblical times. It is no wonder the samovar was so proud.

The tea that the samovar made was warm and wonderful. It was poured forth into our tall glasses at the end of our meal. Yes, tall glasses. That is the traditional way hot tea is served throughout Eastern Europe. My papa had the peculiar habit of keeping a knife in the glass.

I learned how to light the Shabbos candles from Bubby Marcus, who always donned a dishtowel to cover her head for the blessing prayer. She blessed me, too. Her real grandson, Ronald, intoned the ancient recitation of the story of Shabbos, recalling the creation of the world.

I can say, looking back now, that Bubby Marcus was a poor woman by all standards of this world. I can also say that her basement apartment glowed with cleanliness and the pride of keeping one's belongings in order and good repair, no matter how simple. Most importantly, the apartment glowed with the welcoming love of Shabbos—love demonstrated by warm food, *challah* (braided sweet bread), and songs.

Shabbos ended the next evening as the first three stars appeared in the sky and marked the passing of day. A lone silver spice box appeared to be trying to rival the Samovar in his splendor, wafting from its tower the sweet smell of cloves and filling our noses with the fleeting serenity of Shabbos. Bubby Marcus's strange braided candle with many wicks was burning. The darkness of the day now departed was confirmed in the reflection of the candle's light upon our nails before it was extinguished in the wine that had run over from the brimming silver *kiddish* (ritual wine) cup and into the exquisite saucer that held the joy of Shabbos and the sorrow of its passing.

We learned the sanctity of Shabbos at this humble table. Rested and full of prayer and blessings, we understood our heritage. We faced the morrow renewed. We carried forth the sweet aroma of spices, invigorated for whatever the coming days held for us. Yet it is still the strange and lonely sentinel—the samovar—that holds the memory and mystery of a childhood Shabbos remembered with wonder and love.

First Loss

The Sunflowers

Back in the 1950s, Newark was crumbling before our eyes. Not only were the buildings crumbling, but also the social fiber was coming apart at the seams. By 1967, the riots would mark the virtual end of all Jewish life in Newark. Had we stayed there, we would have become a mere thread of what was once a thriving Jewish community. My parents left Newark, among the very last of the Jewish families who had managed to take hold of the American dream. We were all bound for the suburbs, which held the prospect of better schools, greener backyards, and a safer environment for the children.

Did the American dream really hold the promise that Jews could move on to better lives, free from all the cruelties visited upon our people in every generation? My parents wanted to believe that.

This is my story.

Part One: Spring

It was 1955. I was in first grade at Bergen Street School in Newark. Nearing the end of the first term, my parents decided to try to find a new apartment before the summer months arrived, since summertime was when families who wanted to move would most likely try.

Mama found a second-floor apartment in a two-family house located in East Orange on a street of two-family homes called Sunnyside Terrace. A woman of European descent owned the house. Although she initially didn't want to rent the apartment to a family, she agreed to make an exception since I was the only child at home. She told Mama that I would have to wear socks or soft slippers when I was at home because she didn't want to hear footsteps overhead.

When moving day came, my mother seemed extremely tense and edgy, distressed with the fear of annoying our new landlady, Mrs. Riegel.

We walked up the yellow brick steps and through the front door into a small entrance hall with a stained glass window and a tiled floor. The oak door was oiled, and its glass pane sparkled. A faint odor of pine oil hung in the air.

Suddenly the inner hallway door opened, and out popped the landlady. Her appearance quickly dispelled any notion that she might have come to the door to greet us. Her face was anything but welcoming. She wore a cotton housedress, socks, and "sensible" shoes, as my mother called them – laced to the ankle, with thick, squat heels. She appeared to have a moustache. She wore no make-up, and wisps of hair were straggling loose from her bun. My mother would not approve of my unfavorable description of Mrs. Riegel.

The landlady looked down at me with a seriously unpleasant expression. I decided at once that I liked her no better than she seemed to like me. Her welcoming remark was that we were not allowed to use the front door and that we were to be sure to tell my father about this restriction, as she did not want to hear people going up and down the stairs. I heard my mother apologize at least three times.

We went back down the yellow brick steps and decided to take a look at the backyard. It was neat, with trimmed grass and flowerbeds, but there was one thing peculiar about it—in one corner there was a patch of huge sunflowers enclosed by chain link fencing with a gate. The sunflowers were taller than I was. Mama explained that a sunflower looks up at the sun during the day but bends its head when the sun goes down in the evening time so that it appears to go to sleep.

As we turned to leave, we were both startled to find that the landlady had silently followed us out of the house and into the backyard, probably to lay down another rule, I thought to myself. Sure enough, she told us sternly that the yard was not for the tenants and that we were never to open the gate to her sunflower garden or enter it. I decided that I really did not like this landlady or her hideous, hairy, stalked sunflowers. Even at my young age, I thought she made herself like G-d in the Garden of Eden with her forbidden sunflowers. Mama would not have approved of that thought, either.

When Sunday arrived, the landlady went to church. I looked out the window to see what she wore and to see if she still had on one of her flower-printed housedresses. Far from it. In spite of the April sunshine, she had on a woolen coat with a fur wrapped around her shoulders, bundled up as if it were the middle of winter. The fur sported many tails and even the head of a poor pointy-nosed animal. She also wore a felt hat with a foolish feather perched on top of her head. Her thick heels made a clip-clopping noise as she walked across the pavement, and the smell of mothballs lingered in the air when she had passed.

We spent our Sunday unpacking from our move. Tomorrow would be my first day at my new school. The school wasn't far away, and Mama and I had practiced my walk to get there. She had dressed me in a pretty dress she had made, describing to me the whole time how happy the teacher would be to see me. Papa always said that my mother had hands of gold because she was able to make most of my clothing.

"Wait until she hears you read!" Mama kept saying. "She won't believe her ears that a little child can read the way you do!"

The next day I set out alone to face yet *another* first day at school. Just like Mama said, my new teacher, Mrs. Riley, asked me to come up to her desk at the front of the room and read for her to determine in which reading group I'd be placed. I almost smiled when I saw the book; it was a Dick and Jane book I had already finished at my previous school.

The teacher pointed to where I should begin reading. As I read aloud, I glanced up at her and saw that she had a smile on her face. I knew I was reading perfectly. When I finished, she told me that I would be in Reading Group Two. I asked her innocently if that was the best reading group. She told me that it was in the middle.

I went up the back stairs when I got home, remembering the landlady's rule. I put on my slipper socks and went to the kitchen, where cookies, milk, and Mama waited for me.

Mama could hardly wait to hear about my first day. "Tell me all about the reading test," she said. "Did your teacher test your reading?" Her voice was full of anticipation as she waited to hear the good news. "What group are you in? What did she say? Was she surprised at how well you can read?"

"No, Mommy," I said. "I don't think so."

"What, a reader like you?" Mama was surprised. "So what happened? What group are you in?"

"I'm in Reading Group Two."

"What happened to you? Did you make a lot of mistakes?"

"No, Mommy, I don't think I made any mistakes."

"You must have gotten nervous," Mama said. "She'll change your group in no time, when she sees how you can read."

I watched *The Mouseketeers* on television, but their happiness annoyed me. In fact, everyone was too happy. I ate my supper glumly and prepared for school the next day.

Mrs. Riley asked us questions in class, as all teachers do, and of course it was expected that we would raise our hands to answer. I must have raised my hand too much, because she was soon telling me to put my hand down. After that I didn't raise my hand anymore. This continued almost every day, and then she began to order me to put my head down. It was difficult to write with my head down; my eyes couldn't focus at that angle, and I couldn't see what was going on around me in the classroom. To make matters worse, my desk was at the very back of the classroom. Sometimes I would stare off into space, daydreaming, until Mrs. Riley yelled at me to get back to my work. As the days went on, she began to send home any incomplete work for my parents to sign, and she would scrawl "daydreaming" across the top of the papers. Everything was getting worse for me. When Mrs. Riley was on recess duty, she diverted the other children away from me. I would spend most of each recess alone, wondering why Mrs. Riley was so angry with me. I had not yet learned hatred.

I started telling my mother I was sick with stomachaches or headaches; any excuse to stay home.

Mama took me to our trusted Jewish family doctor, Dr. Greenfield, who checked my thyroid, since my mother reported that I was so sluggish and always off in dreamland. Dr. Greenfield told Mama that maybe I was a sort of a morning glory child, who bloomed early and seemed to show intellectual promise at a young age. He told her there was a good chance that I was not as bright as she had first thought. He was our trusted family doctor, and Mama put great stock in any advice from him. I began taking a small white pill called thyroid extract.

Mama let me stay home because I was so miserable at school. She bought me a Ginny doll. Ginny had her own little trunk of clothes and furniture, and I played with her all day long. But Mama knew I wasn't sick, and even though I was still ahead of the rest of my class, she knew it was wrong to keep me at home.

One day, while I was busy playing with my new Ginny doll, Mama sat down on the floor with me and asked what was really wrong with the new school. I finally told her everything—about Mrs. Riley and the way she made me keep my head down, how she didn't let me raise my hand to answer, and about the lonely recess periods.

I don't think it was typical in those days for parents to contact the school superintendent or even the principal to air complaints. My mother sent me back to school, but she showed up at the playground one afternoon, perfectly groomed and classy, as a professor's daughter should be, to see for herself if I really was alone. When she saw that I was, she entered the playground and went up to Mrs. Riley.

"Mrs. Riley," she said, "I am Harriet Ottenstein's mother. I know what you have been up to with my daughter." Before Mrs. Riley could respond, Mama called to me, "Come on, honey, we're going home." We turned and walked off the school property without another word.

My attendance at school for the rest of the term was sporadic. The school year was nearing an end, and summer vacation was just around the bend. Mama's visit to the playground must have had an effect, however, because Mrs. Riley finally let me sit up straight in my chair, and she actually called on me for answers. But my introduction to the sting of prejudice had only just begun.

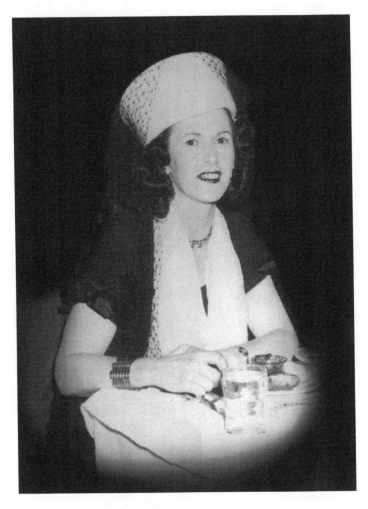

Joan Ottenstein, my mother.

Part Two: Summer

I was lonely. I missed my friends, Moishele, Peter, and Yvette, and especially my best friend Leon. How could we ever have a sukkah in this new home? Would we ever go to the lake or the seashore again?

Next door to us lived a little girl whose family occupied the second floor apartment of another two-family house. The little girl's name was Diane. I asked her one hot June day if we could play when she finished her homework. I waited in the driveway outside her kitchen, listening through the open window to Diane's mother asking her questions from her catechism book. She had to memorize a lot of answers. One of the questions was, "Who is G-d?" I listened to her answer with curiosity, thinking it was odd that anyone wouldn't know who G-d was.

After what seemed like a long time, her lesson was finished, and I called up through the window, "Diane, can you come down and play now?"

"No," she called back. "No, I can't."

"Okay," I said. "Maybe tomorrow?"

"I can't play with you," Diane said. "Go away." Her mother looked out at me and shut the window.

Stunned, I stood frozen in the driveway. Then I did something I was not supposed to do. I walked into the backyard, opened the gate of the forbidden sunflower garden, sat down right in the corner, and stared at the sunflowers' ugly stalks. Dusk had fallen, so they were all looking down at me. I felt my face getting hot as I stared straight ahead, thinking about Diane and her mother.

All of a sudden, I looked up and saw the horrid landlady looking down at me over the chain link fence. I stared blankly at her. She started screaming at me to come out, but I didn't budge. I couldn't. My body felt like it was made of lead. I could hardly even breathe. Mama heard the commotion and came outside right away. The landlady shouted at Mama, telling her how rebellious I was and what a poorly behaved little girl I was. Mama didn't say a word to her, only held out her arms and told me to come to her. It was too much for me to bear. I buried my face in Mama's chest and cried as if I would never stop.

I lay in bed a long time that night, unable to go to sleep. I could hear a group of people whispering some distance away, but I couldn't understand what they were saying, and they seemed to be saying it all together in unison. "Tsa, sa, sa, sa, sa," and again, "Tsa, sa, sa, sa, sa." I was scared, and called out to my mother to come to my room.

"Mama!" I shouted. "Mama, there are voices talking and whispering! They won't go away! They won't stop. Mama! I'm so scared!"

My mother was sitting on my bed. She lunged forward and gripped my shoulders, holding me down. She looked utterly terrified. I'd never seen her look that way before. "No! You don't hear anything! Do you understand me? You don't hear anything! There aren't any voices whispering! Stop it! Stop saying that. There are no voices!"

I continued to cry after Mama left the room. I thought if I kept crying I wouldn't be able to hear the voices. I think a part of me never stopped crying, but I never heard the voices again.

I don't know what happened in the morning, but the voices were never mentioned, and nothing was said about Mrs. Riley, Diane, or the landlady. I think my parents were in a state of fear and uncertainty, not knowing what to do about any of it. They probably hoped and prayed it would just go away.

A few night's later, Mama came into my bedroom and sat on my bed. She told me not to worry anymore and that Papa was going to send me to a Jewish day camp. She said I would have a great time learning how to swim and making friends. An air-conditioned car would take me to the camp in the mornings and pick up other kids along the way. The very best news she had saved for last: we were going to move.

Part Three: Autumn

Just as the leaves were starting to change colors, my mother once again found an apartment on a shady, tree-lined street of two-family houses in Irvington, the next town north from Newark. I would be going to another new school, a one-hundred-year-old building not far from our new home.

Papa would have an easy commute to the produce store where he worked back in the old Jewish neighborhood in Newark, but Mama worried about him. The store was beginning to lose Jewish customers. Uncle Eddie and Papa had to keep their eyes open for thieves; some of the stores in the area had been robbed. Bubby Zelda's neighbor Ida had been beaten in her hallway and left for dead by a man who had followed her home from the grocery store. The old folks in the senior citizen housing were terrorized, having heard her cries but being helpless to do anything except cower behind closed doors and call the police. What made matters worse was that her attacker had screamed expletives and "Jew" as he kicked her, breaking her pelvis and both her legs. He took seventy-seven cents—all she had left in her change purse. This woman had survived the Holocaust, only to be nearly killed in her own home.

Our new neighborhood was inhabited mainly by first-generation Americans with parents from

Poland, the Ukraine, Germany, and Italy. Almost everyone was Catholic. Post war by a mere ten years, these first-generation adult Americans born of immigrants, many of whom still held the biases and prejudices learned from their parents. Though not overtly expressed, anti-Semitism still simmered in the melting pot.

I liked our new first-floor apartment. It had a front porch where I could sit and read or play with my dolls. A friendly couple named Steve and Lucy Sawello were the owners of the two-family house, and they had two daughters, Linda and Kathleen. Linda was almost exactly the same age as I, and we talked excitedly about walking to school together. There were lots of other little girls to play with in the neighborhood, too.

One morning I heard Papa come into the house and whisper to Mama in the kitchen. It might have been the first day of school, but I don't remember exactly. I heard Mama say that maybe I shouldn't go to school. Papa said not to tell me something. My mother didn't always listen to Papa. Looking back, I don't know if this was a time she should've listened, but she didn't. She told me that Papa's car was shot at the night before, and the car windows had bullet holes from a BB gun. Someone had written something ugly on the sidewalk with chalk and drawn an arrow pointing to our house.

I followed Papa outside to see the car for myself. Sure enough, the windows had holes in them like little raised pockmarks. It reminded me of the kind of mark we got from our smallpox vaccinations, with holes in the centers. Papa quickly shooed me back into the house, telling me not to read the words on the sidewalk, but I did anyway. I can still picture them in my mind, even to this day. Beside a long, wiggly arrow and a line pointing to our house, someone had written, "Jews live here."

Linda and I did walk to school together, and we ate lunch together. We were even in the same class. One day on the way to school, we passed by a house with a front porch. Two husky boys were sitting on the steps. They had freckled red faces and red, crewcut hair. Their clunky shoes were dull black. As I passed their house, one cleared his throat in a disgusting way, brought up a great amount of phlegm, and spit it right in my path.

"Dirty Jew," he muttered under his breath.

Linda said something to the boys and pulled me on down the street. "Never mind them," she said. "Their father is a drunk. He beat their mother so much she ran away."

My life-long friend, Linda Sawello-Klappholz, and me.

Part Four: Winter

Life had changed forever, and there was no going back. Certainly there were beautiful Jewish neighborhoods, but those neighborhoods were mainly in
the most affluent areas. Papa was so limited with his
eighth-grade education. At any given time, he had
three jobs to make ends meet, working seventy-two
hours a week. If he could have worked harder or

longer to give us the world, he would have done it. He worked with Uncle Eddy in the produce store, and on Saturday evenings he would work for a friend named Abe Lerner who had a newspaper stand on a busy street corner in Newark. Papa would go to a warehouse and assemble the sections of more than fifteen hundred *Newark Star Ledger* newspapers, then bring those papers to the small covered newsstand and sell the papers all night long, running from car to car in the driving snow and rain. New Jersey winters can be brutal. He also made storm windows and screens for people and carried on a window-washing sideline. These three jobs made it possible for me to go to nice summer camps, take ballet lessons at the respected Lippel School of Ballet, and at sixteen years of age have a Steinway grand piano in our living room. Eventually Papa allowed Mama to go to work, and she secured a job in an exclusive law office in the tower suite of the well-known Raymond Commerce Building. Her income later helped pay for my tuition at the famous Manhattan School of Music.

In this part of Irvington there were few Jews, but I had good experiences at school, and many friends in the neighborhood. Papa took us out for Sunday dinners and bought me an Easter rabbit, which made me immensely popular. However, none of my friends ever knew that I boarded a bus with my sweet public school teacher, Miss Wechter, who made certain I arrived safely to Hebrew lessons. My friend Linda knew that we had special holidays like Chanukah and that Mama kept a kosher home, but no one—not even Linda—knew that we went to *shul* on holidays or that we lit *Yohrzeit* candles (lights or candles to mark the annual remembrance of a death) or that we attended High Holy Day observance with my cousins, Barry and Helene. We took turns in the synagogue, borrowing Uncle Davy's membership seats. Not one of my neighborhood friends knew that we still attended seders held at the Rosenfelds or at Aunt Thelma and Uncle Bernie's house with my beloved cousins Hal, Barbara and Larry.

Chanukah came, proclaiming a miracle. My little menorah, a gift from the Rosenfelds, was set in the center window on the right side of the house. In spite of its miraculous proclamation of victory, it looked so tiny and weak compared to the other houses strung with brilliant colored Christmas lights. Papa gave me a silver dollar on the first night of Chanukah. Mama made her incredible latkes. Papa told me every year how he had searched the whole year looking for the oldest silver dollar he could find so that he could give me a special one each time. I had beautiful *dreidels* (spinning tops), but I soon grew bored of spinning them alone.

That Easter rabbit made me immensely popular.

The Poet Speaks

Chanukah (Dedication)

I can see my menorah glowing in the window
when twilight twinkled on newly fallen snow.
Can you see it beaming across the miles
And remembering you?
The shadows and stars entwined in an embrace.
All was calm as darkness descended upon our city.
Did you see my candle and see me,
Glowing for you, remembering you,
On that night, the first night
of Chanukah?

My candle is a memory of you,
of your light.
I will set you this little candle,
For you who cannot kindle.

Reflections—Reveries

For self-preservation, we lived in a self-inflicted Inquisition. Our Judaism was not public. I think this was a misguided solution and a wrong thing to do. I know my mother orchestrated this secrecy with good intentions on my behalf.

Papa must have been exceptionally lonely. Men in the neighborhood rarely spoke to him. He never joined them in the driveway or on a front porch in the evening when they would talk "man talk" and have a couple of beers after work.

I loved Linda's parents. I spent many happy days at the Jersey shore with her family in their summer home. I believe they loved me. I learned and loved much with the Sawellos—boating, the sea, and fishing. The sea became my life passion. Papa kept the Sawello family stocked with fresh fruits and vegetables and some special meats; it was his way of thanking them for the idyllic summer vacations I would always remember. Mama enjoyed good conversations and coffee with Lucy Sawello, and they became close friends.

The sea became my life passion.

Linda married a wonderful Jewish man, and she remains my lifelong friend. Friends from Florence Avenue School and Irvington High School continue to communicate with me until this day. Auntie Dora talks to me often. I visit her, Leon, and Elizabeth in California, and our conversations pick right up as though we have never been apart. I think we never have.

We moved to Texas to join my brother Allan and his family. A few years previously his employer had transferred him to Houston. His desire was to keep us together as a family. He loved Texas and thought we would, too.

Perhaps time does change things. I would like to believe that. I found this note in my youngest son Daniel's backpack.

A Note. . . from your teacher, Farewell!

You're a very special person,
And, Daniel, you should know
How I loved to be your teacher.
How fast the year did go!
Please come back to visit me
As through the grades you grow.
Try hard to learn all you can.
There is so much to know.
The one thing I tried to teach you
To last your whole life through
Is to know that you are special
Just because, Daniel, you are you!

Rabbi Seymour Rossel and Daniel, my son.

Many guests attended Daniel's Bar Mitzvah, including our congregation, and Ottenstein cousins, Hal, Erik, David, and Aunt Thelma. All had flown to Texas. His classmates, teachers, and neighborhood friends attended, friends of many colors and creeds. They all danced the *hora* (a lively Jewish festival dance in a circle). His brothers lifted him high in a chair in a whirling frenzy of joy. It was a triumph for Judaism, for Daniel, and for my blessed memory of Papa. Most of all, I truly believe it was a triumph for me, for the memory of a Jewish childhood.

But I have never liked sunflowers...

Glossary

Yiddish and Hebrew
Words and Phrases

babushkas: Head scarves.

Bar Mitzvah: Ceremony for a Jewish boy on his thirteenth birthday.

bisel: A little bit.

blech: Metal cover for the stove that could be heated before sundown to keep food warm.

challah: Sweet braided bread, served on the Sabbath; usually two loaves are offered.

Chanukah: Jewish holiday celebrated with eight days of candle-lighting and gifts.

dreidels: Spinning tops that Jewish children play with during Chanukah.

etrog: Yellow citron used on the week-long holiday of Sukkot.

haShem: Literally "The Name", written in place of writing G-d's name.

Hassidim: Ultra-Orthodox Jews who usually wear black coats, full beards and side curls.

hora: Lively circle dance for a festive occasion.

Jashunovka (Jasienowka): Small town near Bialystok.

kiddush: Wine blessing using ritual cup.

knish: Fried dumpling filled with mashed potato.

kvelling: Emoting, raving.

latkes: Potato pancakes made with plenty of oil.

L'chaim: A toast meaning "To life!"

"May she rest in peace": Expression used by religious Jews when mentioning a loved one by name who has died.

lulav: Closed frond of the date palm tree, myrtle, willow and citron which is waved in all directions during the festival of Sukkot.

mechaya: Expression of pleasure, relief.

menorah: Sometimes called *Chanukia*. Eight-branched candelabra used for *Chanukah*.

mezuzah: (plural mezuzot): Small metal or wooden boxes affixed to the doorposts of Jewish homes and containing the most important prayer in Judaism written on a parchment scroll.

mikveh: Jewish ritual bath.

mit da Bristen: With the breasts.

Na: Expression with several meanings. "Aha", or "Now what?", or "See, there it is!"

nachas: Joy, good feeling.

nosh and *schmooze:* Snacks and conversation.

pareve: Neither meat nor dairy. A neutral food.

pogroms: Attacks of pillage and plunder upon Jewish

villages throughout Eastern Europe.

samovar: (Russian) Large copper urn for brewing tea or heating water.

schav: Cold sorrel soup served with sour cream.

schlepping: Dragging with struggle.

seder: Ritual festive meal celebrating the exodus from slavery in ancient Egypt.

Shabbos: Shabbat or Sabbath.

shane madele: Beautiful girl.

Shavuot: Commemorates the anniversary of the day G-d gave the Torah to the people Israel.

shiva: Hebrew for seven. Seven days of mourning. No shaving is allowed, clothing is torn, and mirrors are covered. Referred to as "sitting shiva".

Sholem Aleichem: Famous author of folk stories which inspired the Broadway musical *Fiddler on the Roof.*

shtetl: Small village.

shul: Synagogue.

shvitzing: Perspiring (sweating).

sukkah: Small hut topped with branches to recall the Israelites' wandering in the wilderness. It symbolizes the frailty of life and our dependence on G-d.

Sukkot (Succus): Festival commemorating both the fall harvest and life in the wilderness after we were freed from slavery in ancient Egypt.

Talmud: The most significant scholarly collection of the Jewish oral tradition interpreting the Torah.

Torah: The first five books of the Bible, also known as the Five Books of Moses.

treif: Unfit for eating.

yarmulkes: Jewish skull cap, pronounced by Ashkenazi Jews as *yamaka.*

yenta: Gossiper.

Yiddish: High German language written using the Hebrew alphabet.

yohrzeit: Yearly candle-lighting for beloved dead.

yoi: Expression of woe.

Made in the USA
Lexington, KY
10 September 2012